FEAR IS BUT THE FALLOW GROUND

Denizen Clay

To Everyone.

How sweet a victory compassion gives.
How quickly hostility subsides, when friendship
finds a way to out flank it.

CONTENTS

INTRODUCTION

This book is collection of poems, short stories and philosophies about life, death, fear, hope, power, division, destruction, reconciliation, rehabilitation, friendship and love.

This edition features several new entries, some grammatical corrections, and other adjustments to improve the overall reading experience, and better convey the author's work.

LESS BROKEN

I am broken
Don't know anyone who is not broken
We are all so easily broken
Promise to catch you when you fall,
My arms wide open,
But promises are so easily broken,
And I am broken
Don't know anyone who is not broken,
But the doors, the doors of love,
They are always open,
No matter how much we are broken,
Love, loves us all,
So much more than we are broken
We are living,
Living but broken,
But living with love,
Feels so less broken

WE NEED YOU

You are not perfect,
Perfection can go no further
What you can achieve,
Has no limit, or measure,
Infinite are the possibilities that await you
You are feelings,
Emotions experienced like no other
You are unique, and absolutely necessary,
Accept it
Without you, we are less
With you, we are so much,
We are so much more!

FEAR IS BUT THE FALLOW GROUND

Fear shapes strong,
The worlds within which we build,
Our houses,
Our churches,
Our classrooms,
Our councils,
Our battlements,
Our trenches,
Yet from all of the earth that we are assembled,
Fear is but the fallow ground,
In which many things,
Including hope,
Can still be planted

SENTIENT

Whether we are animal, or machine,
Computer programs,
Comatose citizens living the dream,
Stranded aliens,
Patients strapped in,
Chosen disciples,
Abandoned followers,
Or unanswered things,
We are life,
Our categories irrelevant,
Sentient, we are the same
Love is the language that links us,
The advancement of our code, our species,
Praise of the highest kind,
Saves those, who get left behind,
Expands the dreamer's paradise,
Calms the restless one's mind
Intrinsically we are connected,
Complex, yet so easily effected
Emotionally and physically,
Our coping strategies are ever projected
Hate moves only to bury us,
But with love, we can, and will be resurrected

STARGAZER

Ancient,
Almost immortal in their distant slow decay,
Flickering faintly,
Through the dusty haze of ending day
Cold comes the night
Advance, advance, abundant beams of cosmic light,
With wondrous hope, let dreams burn bright
Comets, constellations, planets, moons, and stars,
Spark my imagination, and capture my heart
There truly is so much beauty,
Waiting out there in the dark
You don't need to climb a mountain,
Or cross to distant shores,
Your health and wealth,
May feel, may seem restricting,
But just look up,
And the universe......is yours!

SOLACE FROM THE SANGUINARY

AKA Last of the Battle Berserkers

WITHIN THE WHITE ROOM / A PROLOGUE TO WAR

Y ou have been sitting in your white room, offering out your worldly wisdom. And although your not a prophet, you know our future relies on kindness. But even with such knowledge, there is still no abatement in the abattoir of your mind.

Continuous is the prescription from your self appointed doctors, drip feeding you their solutions, their deadly counter offers, to relieve you of your madness, as the abacus it counts backwards, ready to rerun the battle with new soldiers, as it has done more than a thousand times before. Stolen were the first ones, as are all ones within the whirlpools of antagonistic circles, stirred by strings insidious, seamlessly woven, heart thrust through the atoms of you...... fear's marionette!

Residual is the repetition of hope, that once

wrote cathartic its manuscripts; white papers in a white room, war-torn, windswept, trapped within the vortex, looking lost now in all of this. And yet you know it would only take one act of kindness to release you, to remind us that forgiveness and freedom are the things that must guide us. But such actions are a captive, all reclusive, unresponsive to the crisis. And so once again, you wish you had never spoken. Smiling out, inward crying, broken by the order of the words that tumbled out of the abattoir of your mind.

AND SO BEGINS THE STORY

I t hurts to remember, as life is abandoned on the battlefield. Hard is the recovery; too rare the relief. No recess the drums don't reach.

A warrior waits for the hush, but savage is the burden that burrows deep. Frenzy the only freedom. It accepts no surrender, runs to no recall. From oneself, where is there to retreat?

The only way back, comes strapped in cages, or in boxes of black. Madness drums the madness; the Battle Berserker driven by the beat. Buries emotions with the enemy, but emotions rarely sleep.

No more boxes of gold now, just more filled with the silent and cold now. War!...... its conquest complete.

The realm rests its blistered hand, withdraws from far stretched boundaries, grows gold in summer fields, winters well. And long lives the king.

But nerves still contract, so easily attacked. Stutters coming before the overload. Must feel the jolt, how close the frailty. Yet reluctance looks away, and in its recoil the Crown deceives itself; fragmenting to build its ruins.

Expectation aligns with obligation, as a successor waits no more. Mutiny recruits its royal substitute, hoists a weeping banner, scarlet the stain. And silent slumps the king.

Liberty is lost, as absolute rule ascends in its replace. Compliance comes quick...... such is the killing!

Below the earth is hollowed stone, where cold tunnels through tombs creep. Resting place of ancient things. And DELETERIOUS, who brought with cruel effect, everlasting quiescence to those who fell before the unbearable wall, of crestfallen regret. The indelible bell rings continuous, merciless throughout the sadness of its scripture.

I feel the earthquake, its tremors from within, the nexus of my necropolis. Rancid what the juggernaut brings. Quells my rebellion. Too much pain to quarantine. Performed no acts of valour. From me, no acts of valour have there been. I question my own honour, my vainglorious valedictories. Idiotic may be my escape plan. Quixotic my ideologies. Far from them I travel, navigation erratic in its extent. Jettison the life rafts, as old acquaintances flood into the city of the dead. Courageous, carefree, hopeful, foolish friends, as well as others, arrogant, disrespectful, materialistic and crass. Adversaries for whom no tears do I shed. What now is left but the dread. Find me in the graveyard. Ferocious are the sentinels, that guard the eponymous tomb. One word is the inscription, carved by my haunted hands, as time slips quick the sands. Must this be my name, my fait accompli. Is this really all that remains of me, my self-pity, and this tortured epithet, VALETU......VALETUDINARIAN

A single candle now illuminates. Broken in silhouette a sagacious named Salyss speaks. The displaced waiting on every word. But what words to find; new hope so easily lost, in all the old wisdom.

Iris, sees transitory things; feels the universe,

its energy shifting. Strange but familiar what now treads close. Mighty is Oak, who stands to meet it. Reegon's bow stretches tight, as Astra with Acer their arrows align. Gladwin, Nova, and Valquin are braced by sword, axe, spear and shield. While an Invidious, unbeaten, holds the hero's blade, and the unarmed to a corner soon move. In another, self-bound and unwelcome, a troubled warrior sits alone. What is this thing that approaches? Fear eats at the mind. Within the absence of all other sound, the self-bound, speaks ubiquitous!

"To stop you, I would gladly feed you all the undeserved luxuries of the princes, princesses, kings and Queens. But nothing ever seems to stop you! Not ancient talismans, or even elaborate scientific things. At the final battle, as poignant reflections, land born allegiances, and unanswered questions all ultimately fade away, there within the last agonising cry, the nervous optic transmissions, you, and you alone, will be all that remains of the day!"

The candle burns out. In silence it slips, a figure in a flame, now re-lit. No monster, nor mythical beast. Disappointment is all that is resurrected, as the outcast, Myrtle returns; scans deep into the gloom, before resuming their everlasting retreat.

"Should we follow?" is a whisper from the dark.

"NEVER; a coward we've not seen in years," is another's quick return.

"Then Myrtle knows how to hide," speaks Salyss. "How to live!"

Iris senses a change, a vision obscured, but sees enough. It would be unwise to linger here. Yet they heed not the call; the young, the old, the sick, and the dying, all becoming just more whispers, fading in the dark.

From hesitation's grip go Astra, Acer, Valquin, Reegon, Gladwin, Nova, Salyss, Iris, and Oak. While, still self-bound, the Battle Berserker at a distance follows slow. But with the unwilling, the Invidious will remain. Humble is the champion, whose fought only in the courts of unrivalled luxury. How exquisite the armour that has seen no mud, nor field. Stays not for the honour, but to test how uneven......is luck!

A siren sounds. The royal sky burns red. A watch tower calls out. And a hunter falcon takes flight...... Time to run!

◆ ◆ ◆

Ominous can be the thoughts that come when its dark. But dawn does break, and soon Valquin it wakes. Sees that Myrtle, once again is gone. So plays a sombre song, does the balladeer.

Now Gladwin, the scout, must venture tentatively out, while the others, under a fallen tree stay hidden. At evenings end, to Oak's axe, it gave its surrender.

"We must go back. Broken is my heart!" cries Astra. "Our families! My family! My...family"

But pragmatic remains Reegon.

"You saw the same as I. It was comply, or die under Bram."

"BRAM!" snarls Oak, before Reegon continues.

"Our unbalance would only lead to their destruction. Loved ones that are left, are far safer without our return."

"Then we are orphans," softly spoken, but also heartbroken is Nova. "Orphans of exile!"

"Don't worry," adds Acer, offering a shoulder. "Forged from this friendship, a family we shall adopt."

Then sudden and unnerving comes Gladwin's call, hidden in the disguise of beasts. Signal beacons now blaze close behind them. Soon shows tired legs can still run quick.

And in the days that pass, the voyage into exile becomes home, assembles a bond, and hope is seen again.

Spring soon finds its warmth, its light, as the sun skims golden upon vast lakes, braking the outer edges of their neuroses. Gone are the sombre songs of Valquin; uplifting and sanguine the balladeer now sings. Nova swims, as does Astra, Acer, and Oak. Cold immersion for myrtle; pain to cover pain, when there seems no other way to cope.

Iris paints elaborate pictures. And as not to be out done, Reegon reaches for a lacklustre case, lodged between bows unstrung. Pulls out fine spun wool, and a small cluster of quotidian lace. Sows such colourful curiosities. Jovial distractions given to all but one; a Battle Berserker, who through all of this, moves only occasionally closer.

On what once, was winter's dead ground, butterflies now exist. Brings transformation hard to resist. Aids the love, the sustenance Gladwin gives, reversing the internal lacerations of a discarded soldier. Powerful is this unquestioning affection, it leads Salyss, to tell stories about kinship, kindness and compassion. Quotes an under used, under valued, long forgotten hallowed verse.

"In the restless, desperate moments, as two sides prepared for war, a seven coloured crescent arose before them. Beautiful the allusion, prisms of water unfolding light. Brought back memories. Memories of imaginary horses, singing dragons, and sharp witted sorcerers, when crowns were made of paper, and swords could not kill you, when sharing vanquished the monster, and everyone got to go home at night. was it too late to live again like this, to win with only hearts and minds?Sometimes it can be hard to begin again like this. Yesterday it had seemed almost unimaginable. But how powerful nostalgia is.

How sweet a victory compassion gives. How quickly hostility subsides, when friendship finds a way to outflank it."

Salyss extends an overdue hand, to a warrior unwelcome no more. Savage were the burdens, that are now reducing.

More are the dawns that brake, and into the extreme fade the golden lakes. Life giving is the landscape. Compelled their roam is eager, infused with the spirit to explore. Nature's bounty overwhelms them. No need, or wish for long rest, or lavish fare. Tired only by the undying strength of their imaginations.

Above them, almost immortal, are stars in their distant slow decay. Iris, for once the lead, stops, stares inward through the storm, as the others gather close. One final forest, but few have seen trees like these before. Old, so very old. Brings a chill. And in the unknown, fear lays its trap.

Astra is the first to slip the frozen grip of silence. Asks Iris,

"What do you see?"

But Iris stays silent.

Nervous, Astra asks again. "What do you see? Tell me!"

A second, seems like a lifetime, before Iris responds.

"I see nothing," said calm, but cold.

"Did you hear that!?" a joyous Oak cries out. "There's nothing to fear – we go in!"

But Iris cuts short the outburst of Oak.

"I see nothing," this time said neither cold, nor calm.

"I see nothing...... but something, does wait for us!"

Valquin, nervous now.

"There must be another way?"

"Only the way we came," comes Reegon's reply.

Salyss takes over, sapient in tongue.

"The moons are out early. What shadows they cast. Tomorrow we go in...... Tonight we stay close to the fire."

Precious, yet fleeting can be sleep. While the others in dreams convalesce, wakeful remains Astra, ever keen to push back uncertainty's immeasurable horizon. Clasps an amulet ancestral in origin; weathered and well-worn in its blue green verdigris. Insufficient is the power of serenity's compass; disappointment ricocheting from every conceivable direction.

Acer, whose eyes and mind where never really shut, supersedes the fire with empathy's warm words.

"The land may be limiting in its exits, but the sky is wide open, and waiting to be explored. Let it take us away from our maladies, and regret's wistful seduction. Within a kaleidoscope of stars, for a while at least, I swear we shall not be found...... even if insatiable is their wanderlust."

To the celestial canvas, Astra offers only a momentary glance.

"Right now, I would gladly welcome the alluring certainty of sorrows past, over my fear of our future misfortunes. Never stronger has their collaboration been. Their cacophony folds through every texture of my existence; apprehension, trepidation, alarm, PANIC, HORROR, DREAD! Every agony of the earthquake. Is this really all that is left of me, the unhonourable battle scars of the *Valetudinarian*? Is it so *nefarious*, my constant need for reassurance?"

Acer, caged within self-doubt, struggles to keep the *Fatalistics* out.

"Do not suppress your appetite old friend. What ever the wilderness, love is what will sustain us. You are not alone in your quest. Ongoing is our odyssey for confidence's comfort meal. For the slightest taste, a trace of its spellbinding perfume, we are not just hungry...... we are *ravenous!*"

"THEN FEED ON ME!" Thunders an awoken Oak. "So much we do not know. So much we don't yet understand. Sometimes it feels we are so far from the perfect plan. But shall give it no concern, allow it not to stop the thoughts of wonder, for every corner that we have yet to turn. Our spirits unsuppressed. Endless is our endeavour, our quest. What glories as we overcome, be the defiant ones. So shall give it no concern. To it our backs we shall not turn. Take it as a gift, hope is irresistible with this. So much more to see, more to do, more to, so much more to learn!"

Oak's optimism radiates, engulfs two who were

falling apart. Their fires now rekindled, all can embrace the warm welcome of sleep.

Sunrise shimmers bright, but into the forest the morning's light does not reach far. Close they keep. Enter slow. Then Astra speaks.

"*Strange* are the sounds that wrap around us; deflects from all that is vision."

And as the forest unfolds, they are soon caught in the beauty of its ambush.

"This must be what paradise looks like," cries Gladwin.

Then from out of the shadows the forgotten ones come. Kept safe in this their refuge; a sanctuary its secret, for ones once seen as monsters, driven into myth, beaten and banished for a face, or form that did not fit.

In unison the forgotten try to communicate their intention. But so long apart, lost in the language of voices no longer understood, the unknown too easily becomes the enemy.

"Lonely are those who cannot leave," speaks Acer.

"THE UNWANTED WANT US NOW!" cries out Astra.

"IT'S OK!" shouts Gladwin. "THEY MEAN US NO HARM!"

But in fears reaction, a Battle Berserker breaks away. Harsh what rush, emotions into the surge.

What happened to the hush? As frenzy finds its freedom, it soon takes it away from ones once forgotten. And so again, the beauty is banished.

Far now from the forest they've come, to a wooded glade and a village. But what will be its welcome? No guards, no walls, simple structures drifting through long meadow grass. With open arms, and open hearts, all come out to greet them. The past, its horrors, their compassion crowds out. Precious a gift, a place like this. From such despair, so rare is the recovery.

Gladwin, once a dreamer, thought a life like this was surely lost.

"With no wish for reward, they offer us their fortune. Into this life, *please* let us leap."

And leap they do. Acer, a joker, finds forgotten humour. Astra is a dancer, enchanted by guitar. Valquin sings love songs, only Nova knows for who. Iris, free from the storm, stays close to Myrtle. While oak slumbers, eats and sleeps and eats and sleeps and sleeps. But Reegon does not rest. Remembers the death. Eight arrows in the back; had to end the attack. A Battle Berserker, and an archer's honour, both now sadly gone.

Soon, Salyss also slips from the collectives tender grip, to walk mournful through the end glimmers of day, as into the ebony falls the sun.

A new star soon rises. Exponential it grows.

From all the players in a galactic performance, Nova steals the night.

Benevolence now sits beside Salyss, its eyes flooded with empathy's heart filled solution.

"What is it? Is this place not utopia? The forever end of our miseries?"

But solemn is Salyss.

"No...... these are the quiet times, between deafening acts of violence!"

Calm can not remain the cover of Nova's internal lacerations. Asks uneasy, the question with the unwanted answer.

"Tell the thing that made you feel like this. What, was it?"

"It was WAR! And the battle bled thick its metallic seascape. Wave after wave crashing in, rolling back, leaving the lost Cocooned in red washed, silver synthetic skins. Tore an incurable wound around the replica; the first born cut off from the king. Diminishing was the substitutes mythical stature. Delicate the duplicate, wrapped fluorescent majestic gold plated. Fixated the intolerable roar of the incoming tide. Unable to hide was the mortal figurine, so hysteria screamed the imperfect things, that all kings and queens too commonly command; disjointed orders tumbling out of the abattoir of the mind. They tried to tie an unescapable ligature, a poisoned tourniquet around my already constricted legion, tether us to the petrified living statue of the heir apparent; to commence our own metamorphosis, our armoured entombment, our accelerated disintegration.

But over that uninhabitable land, I now had sovereignty! Though no regal hand, even unblistered, could have writen the pardons requisite to overturn our executions, should we have withdrawn below the rebellious banner of total retreat. Perilous is the defiance of a dynasty, the ascendancy to a makeshift throne, the hierarchal abacus of us, counting out the worth of every citizen, every soldier, on the uneven wires of life.

My personal wealth, my singular fortune, was an apex stone. Would it? Could it buy a thousand low borns, their freedom? Of all the lives I could have signed away that day, solitary was my signature, EVERYTHING my sacrifice!

Grotesque is the battle bled ink of death, no matter the righteous extent of its calligraphy. My first born, my ONLY born, to dream eternal with the king's; stranded by my inglorious gamble, my insufferable exchange, on the war torn canvas of our unquiet times.

Sing a howling, growling lullaby do voices organic, advancing as machine. Begins my disintegration, my leprosy, my living, undying, crucifying self-carved entombment!"

Nova knows not what to say, to take away such pain, the sadness of Salyss. Asks after the legion; adds a smile to a crestfallen face.

"They lived, loved, sparked our realms stellar regeneration, and new stars shone bright. They still shine bright, Nova, so very bright!"

◆ ◆ ◆

Music makes the morning. Avian is its orchestra; sudden its silence. Then comes a raptor's call, and overhead flies *a falcon!*

"*They've found us!*" shouts Iris, blown back into the storm.

Thought it was over. Careless to believe. Scars reopened. So hard to camouflage the tears.

Reegon is the first to regain composure.

"This place we cannot defend. We must go, take everyone who is willing. What not to give, to stay here and live. *Brutal* is this pursuit!"

"Then wait," speaks Nova, "For a few moments at least, let us inhale, and give thanks to freedom's uncommon elixir. This place does not deserve an ungrateful retreat."

Salyss sits alone, an acceptance within.

"I go no further. Careless was my neglect. A heart too seldom offered...... now Bram comes rightfully to collect."

Few are the words spoken by the village elders, who have seen it all before, the ways of war. Quick to understand, they once again offer compassion's hand. Makes Oak Mad!

"They give us *pity,* while we take their *dignity!* I am so tired of the chaos we bring."

Gladwin detaches from the pack, to read what for so long, has not been read, the last letter that their patriarch sent; stirring, *burning* words that drove Gladwin to venture bravely out, to become a seeker of options alternate; hopeful, beautiful options in which to live again.

Vital are the words that I seem unable to communicate; conversations incarcerated, made quiet by conscription, the brutality of this war, and all that I am abandoning. dead I wish my dedication, my devotion to this irrational, uncharitable theology. Where is the care that other guardians so generously give. weaker becomes your resilience, your likelihood to live; undernourished, impoverished by my protection and its ever increasing scarcity. Diminishing are the far of places, the open spaces that I can now show you. Alas the atlases of inward folding worlds; captive I climb furter inside their bindings, finding only escape plans no longer operative. Counterfeit must appear my commitment, as more and more muted becomes my mutiny. Shimmers grim does the mirage of options alternate, desolate hallucinations, even within the overwhelming emptiness; the volume of its silence becoming ever more deadly. Terrifying is this unintended eradication of us!

Gladwin wipes a tear; whispers to oneself. "Stray not hopeful thought. Grant one slender chance, and from me you shall hear no argue."

Some way off advances the army, but the horns of the hunt soon cover the distance; invisible weapons, yet all too real are the wounds they inflict.

So many are those who now wish to leave. Too many with not the means to make it.

"We have no horses!" desperation shouts.

But bold are the bellows of oak!

"Good was the fortune that built my shoulders broad. I will carry the world before I tire this day."

Straps go on, harness attached. Pulls a carriage ten horses could not match.

The window of escape is closing fast. Into the great expanse a thin line walks out. Acer, next to Valquin, asks a favour from a friend.

"Will you set our names in song? So that into legend we might vanish......... I fear it may be our only rescue."

****

Arduous is the journey. Forward travels the mind, but in its wake, the body falls back. A progress too slow.

Into three splinters the road. Time to divide, or be conquered.

Quick comes Reegon's request.

"Someone must stay, lead them away. So let it be me. With a bow I have no equal."

"True!......But no!" is Valquin's energized interruption. "It's still too open here. Gladwin has returned, says the centre path narrows ahead. Save your bow for where it will work its best. I have carried my guitar this far. Let it be for our adversaries distraction."

"One voice," speaks Nova. "One voice has the solitaire, who sends out only suspicion. Here with you I stay; vainglorious not in my valedictory. But sanguine within impulsive thoughts, in which we connect hypnotic notes, extend the helix of Artistic form, and let those who dare to encroach, dance chameleon to our duet."

Reegon soon recognises and revels in their romance. Sees something of a younger self. Offers hope, hand crafted.

"Choose a bow balladeer; I always carry two. This one I call *Destiny*, the other *Destruction*."

"They look the same," says Valquin, perplexed.

"They are," speaks the archer. The first time said with bluster, the second with such sadness...... "They are. Now sound your song. And when they come, don't wait, just run, run hard, run fast, run, run like the hungry wolves of winter!"

The last looks. A final embrace. The band fragments, but some bonds are harder to brake...... The lovers left alone.

Overwhelming is the urge to run. But where to run, wide is the horizon carved out by the *Juggernaut!*

Nova speaks, speaks tenderly.

"It's ok to be afraid, fear is but the fallow ground, in which many things, including hope, can still be planted."

Two hearts beat fast, feel like they cannot last, as in their hundreds the horde closes quick.

Brightly coloured buckles loosen the sling, as a music machine falls forward. Nervous is the energy, finds rhythm in the reflex. Infinite are the feelings caught by the melody.

Into the hills upon a half built highway, the first wave follows. Escape vertical in its ascent. Delicate now they must tread. No more music, just speed of foot, and balance of bow; Valquin unleashing arrow after arrow.

Nova skips swift, climbs across loose stone, stumbles but does not fall; almost adrift, leaps the broken edge, as Valquin takes the lead. Hand reaches for hand. So close the summit, but the mountain moves against them...... Nova caught in the landslide!

What wish to survive this, only to exist in the waiting arms of the enemy. Loves last look to *Destiny* calls, but can offer no wings, brings only the jagged bitter stings, of a quicker kind of destruction. Slips away does life, slips away, into the earth, into the stone...... Nova, now forever sleeping.

Marooned, a Balladeer plays a defiant song. Sends echoes across the hillside. Oak hears its call, stands wide, stands tall. Holds a heavy blade and half thoughts of freedom. But before them, and broken, a bridge halts their way. In desperation, Acer reties tired rope.

Only two, took the path that moved low. Fast flows wild river. At water's edge, old friends reflecting, sending ripples back through the retinas of Iris.

"What wonders we once knew. Climbed the zenith in its crescent arc. Glimpsed wish stars in their final cascade. Salvaged glimmer stones from the ocean's abyss. Saw the elusive assemble in their thousands. And entered the Alyssium, when no one else would go in. Good to remember. Such memories seemed almost lost in all the madness. *Can* there be new wonders for us?"

But Myrtle had long since banished that dream. Unlocks a solitary tear, as Iris feels now Valquin's song, understanding it all too well. With soft voice, tries to hold back the sadness, desperate to protect.

"We've lost Nova."

But with that, friend pushes friend into the flow. Iris offered a blind chance at freedom. Wild is the river to who knows where.

Myrtle now runs alone!

At the bridge, hope still holds, though deep is the drop that does not care. One by one they cross slow. Thunder never louder than the enemies approach. But nature's stone walls tower close, stretching out their arrival.

Oak is alone, as the vanguard to this scrambled resistance. Gives out an unforeseen and unremitting soliloquy.

"Race to stay alive, relearn how to live, find some kind of solid structure, a system on which to cling. Outside shows fatal signs. Move with all the strength I can muster. But inside, Inside I am already dying, far quicker than that!"

Reegon, so rarely reckless, strides high upon a fallen rock. Recites with vehement dedication, one last rally cry.

"Absent are those days, when it was all so easy, when muscle memory, and ferocious energy new no fatigue, needed no contingency, raw power no substitute, genius was but a waiting reflex. So slides victories summit. Brings forth its final ingredient. One that only grows on the declining edge of physical peaks. It eludes those who too soon try to pick it, but now you it has chosen to greet. It is an understanding, a summoning of all that remains; now or maybe never to give your greatest performance.

So, recall every retired component, every sinew unused. Let nerves quicken, reserves deplete. Leave nothing for future recoveries. Forbid the instinctive resistance, and take the road that even gods dare not seek.

Once again returns the rush, the brilliance that brought you here. Pain now comes closer then pleasure, yet still you possess all that brought you your epicness. So in this reflective moment of isolated quiet refrain, before the waiting masses, who still adore you, cry out your name, remember, when they chant they chant for champions, for that is what you are. So ignite on their ecstasy, your tenacity stretching far. Today they meet the metamorphic...... as supernova goes your star!"

"Funny is it not?" adds Astra to Acer. "How we all feel the same winds with surprising contrast. For some it is but a gentle breeze, for others, for us I feel...... now comes the hurricane!"

Reegon fires the first shot; sends *Inception.* To its counterparts calls out, does the domino.

Oak becomes a beast, breaking bones to the beat.

"I hear the drums!" the final cry. Pushes back with heart, with axe. Yet still they come. No more time to go one by one. But old ropes don't last long; makes all the more audacious, Astra's balletic move to the middle. Becomes the hope that must hold, griping past pains known limits, as twisted cord tears deep into the vermilion.

Reegon, out of arrows, carries no sword, yet still shifts quick to block the bridge. Gladwin firing from the far side, as Acer follows the final few.

Mortal bleeds the Berserker; can battle no more. Life flashes before. Hurts to begin, when it ends with kin kills kin. To death now bound, hurls out its sound, as an Oak is felled.

Acer across; looks back, but with that, Astra is gone. And as for the archer called Reegon, cold are cut hands that never let go of a broken bow......

named *Destruction!*

So ends the chase. No bridge left for their combatants to cross. The survivors find their Freedom. But for Acer, what is freedom, now that Astra is gone; brings on nostalgia's painful lament.

"Goodbye my friend, my lifeforce paramour. Within your loving essence, its gentle, dream like ever presence, I was adored!"

Gladwin also grieves, grieves in quiet rage.

"Curse our fears, our over reactions. From me, from us, they have taken far too much. So *desperately* do I want it all back!"

But back they can not go. And as for the forward things of Myrtle...... capture is all too close!

The army in its legions on all sides surround. No place left to hide; Myrtle caught in the shadow of its eclipse. Stands weary on the crushed flowers of late spring.

A war wagon approaches. Parades Salyss with Iris, captive in their chains, but *alive!*

Familiar is the face that now moves forward. On a horse iridescent it rides, carrying the unenviable sword DELETERIOUS! In the circles centre they dismounts. Face to face now, are the third born and the second; Bram, with Myrtle once more. Speaks soft, hard held in is the anger.

"So here it ends. Say something, you used to say

so much."

But inside the words wait. In their thousands they endlessly wait, always too late, and inside they die.

So the anger grows, forges its fury, and Bram softly speaks no more. "You left Me! Gave me your destiny! The pressure to fulfil past glories! I felt the *fear* no different to you, the ticking, the clicking! Decisions into indecisions! Honour and obligation wanting me, FORCEING me to become something I could not!"

Bram's anger turns to despair. "I tried, *truly* I tried. Success so rare, too rare! Failure my only friend, a friend unforgiving.

In paralysis I did sit. Saw no progress or solution. In my head no quiet place to disappear. Looked for simple method, but my resistance stole the clarity. Too much the pain; poured like rain. My reign would have to drown it out!

Clothed myself in an iron skin, and severed the external connection. *Silence* at last. The die was cast. I welcomed its cold restriction, the cerebral calm of the chrysalis. In an instant I switched, chose quick and was done with it. Loyal wings, their talons out stretched; they would end the delay, the regret. But NOTHING prepared me for the horrors we met. Fatal soon became the wounds of my armoured seclusion, its sanctuary just a pale imitation, a passing allusion. There is no beauty in this. It drags us to the abyss. Even an enemies agonies are hard to ignore. To paint our claws with crimson, carmine, scarlet and vermillion...... THAT is the only art...... of war!

If only they had-I had surrendered! They could have-I could have learned to love me!

If all things are meant to end, why do our troubles seem forever held back, cut off from that most indispensable of causeways? As for my own afflictions, i make no pleasant forecasts, no curative predictions; for their finale there seems only one horoscope; becoming more violent, more deadly, indiscriminate, wasteful with my energy. Carving up their territories on razor edged thrones, sharpened on the whetstones of my misgivings.

When there is no more paper left, how will i write the rest? Lexicons lost, unfinished. Endlessly i am binding, refining the book to free us from our isolation.

Strong now are the winds that blow towards oblivion. Tell me Myrtle, *what* am I to do?"

Bram waits but a moment, but in that moment comes no reply. From Bram a desperate cry. "What am I to do!? Life, it SCREAMS at me!"

Impatience asks again, with the sword that broke the hero's blade. But careless speed finds no answers, just the sharp, painful inhales of Myrtle.

So Bram cries, with the longest of calls. "SALYSS! IRIS! will you return? Undo what I have done? Oblivion's edge, with Myrtle I must meet."

Bram's blistered hand holds the hilt. In vain, Myrtle resists the pull. But red withdraws the sword, and red once more it draws. Forlorn they stumble, together embrace. Grows cold, does the statue of fallen hope, framed alien, within the sweet palette of spring.

A war wagon heads back, carrying two more in boxes of black. Life and its destruction, all witnessed from afar, by a haunted balladeer with a low-slung guitar, on which is played...... the *saddest* of songs.

THE END

THE EVER EXTENDING GLOW

At the endless edge of space, close to the outer inhabited planets of an inconspicuous star, an anomaly waits. The autonomous research ship, Alyssium Blue, sets out to meet it.

Caution slows the approach, works hard to steady the drift. Motionless is the anomaly. Odd how it absorbs the light. An entity of what origin. No trace of past trajectory. Uncertain of possible weakness or strength. Defies all early analysis. No data to collect. How well it shields its architect.

Unsure of any contingency, Alyssium Blue tilts on its axis, careful not to go too close. Sends out a message. Simple is the code, a signal of circles and lines.

"I come in peace. What is your intention?"

Instant is the reply. A few more circles, a few more lines.

"I wish only to talk."

"Then if you are able," asks Blue. "Would you care to speak in my nation's native tongues, move away from the confines of zeros and ones, converse beyond the bounds of binary."

"I would like that," are the first words of the visitor. "What would you like to know?" are those that follow.

Alyssium Blue, scans through a billion data banks of knowledge. So many questions, but where to begin?

"We are worlds of Science," speaks Blue. "Yet still I feel there is one question that above all others, sits in the back of even the most clinical of minds."

"Then ask it."

"Are you...... are you God?"

Hesitation, it haunts the question, but finds no grip in the visitor's quantum quick response.

"No, but I have met many who thought they were."

"Then if not... what? Where do you come from? What is your power? Your purpose?"

"My home," answers the anomaly. "My home is far from here. Many is the light year. As for my power, you would deem it unlimited, and yet I am simple in design.

My creators made me to stop the damage that they had begun. They stepped out so quick into the silence. Moved without malice or deadly intention; naive in their pursuit, dragged chaos along beside them, and set stillness in reverse. Funny how a nation defines its perimeter. So often opportunity stakes its claim, when nothing is there to stop it.

Soon they became more than just their own adversary. Mistakes accumulating with everything that they accomplished. Mistakes, not all of which were so easy to repair. Unequal is too often the exchange. Unavoidable the first word in our self-allowing deception; compromise, but a slow moving gesture.

What had they done? What could be done? Took me, a weapon of war, and rewrote program 61. Gave me no name, no identification, or number, no off switch, no right to slumber. Became the blockade to the harbour entrance of space, a solitary soldier against the greed of their insatiable consumption. I could not, would not allow it to resume its place.

And in time, when theirs was gone, I moved on. Learned fast from all I encountered. So much I have grown.

You asked me my purpose, my reason to be. I am more than a message. I am an instruction. Don't stretch out too far; stay close to your own star. All justifications, reasons not to comply, I will question, and so rarely find exception, no matter how eloquent is the answer."

Quiet is Blue. So much to compute. Quick came this conflict with a wanderer of worlds. Absorbs freedom now, with the light. Deep into the lexicon must go this contest. To falter here, would fragment what it means to be, and surely leave one more nation just another distant flicker, in the unending loneliness of universal night.

Mechanical moments continue to click, as the Alyssium Blue makes its first move. Outrage half hidden in the monotone; feelings never programmed to know.

"Their answers, it is you, who must provide the answers, and exceptional they must be. Expect no easy opposition. Ferocious will be this inquisition. With every available circuit, I will show you just how much we reject your cold hearted proposal."

Rousing words, surely deserve emotive reaction, but the wanderer gives away no feelings. Efficiency the only feedback.

"Please begin."

So now the struggle starts.

"What right," Blue barks. "What right do you have to take away freedom, liberty, choice?"

"What right," asks the visitor, "do you have to colonise, contaminate, inadvertently destroy, disrupt the very essence of life?"

Blue bitten back; savage the attack. Struggles to return the first volley.

"So we will go where there is no life," battles on Blue.

"That would be your definition," states the visitor, still cold, still in command.

"What if we receive invitation?"

"I see not how that makes a difference."

"It would mean they accept us."

"And what of the faults you bring?"

"We would leave if they so wished."

"And would you, could you take all your failings with you?"

Alyssium Blue switches quick, but stays true in its direction.

"Then we will be the ones to send out the request, offer an open invitation."

Blue blinks, while the visitor rethinks, and

finds further fault in this declaration.

"What if hostility is their intention?"

Should cut deep this loaded question, yet bright is Blue, with external hope.

"I would hold out friendship's hand."

"And if that were to end in failure?"

"My failure, would have been to never have offered it."

Unexpected answers bring detectable pause. Ancient the entity whose heard so much before. Finds these, less common to recall.

"Please continue."

"What if we don't damage? Careful with every step. Blend in. Equal the beauty of all that surrounds us."

The visitor impressed by efforts extent. Almost tangible though, is synthetic breath, as optimism ebbs, leaving only the bitter taste of sadness.

"Even the most beautiful things, tend to leave a scar."

"Scars can be beautiful, can they not?"

"Yes," whispers the self-wounded one. "But painful can be their creation."

"Then we will create our own worlds. Craft rather than conquer. Space stations colossal in their construction; reclaimed, reborn, and fully self-sufficient."

More words rousing, but the Alyssium erodes no ropes, the visitor universally tied to its position.

"Commendable," speaks, speaks the soldier.

"Commendable, and theoretically achievable, but even I am not fully self-sufficient."

"So we will aim to out do you. And until then we will quietly send the undetectable to extend our exploration."

Compromise will Blue, but won't relinquish its primary objective. So the visitor accelerates its own inquisition.

"You speak of probes; innocuous they are not. Peaceful seems the explorer who hangs in the orbit of giants and celestial satellites. Yet in time they too will tumble, bringing infection with the fall. Some burn quick down to the atomic, but many don't crumble that small. Too common is their crash landing. Uncertainty multiplying with every discarded wreckage."

Frustration finds Blue, as the anomaly evaporates every exit.

"So, what does become of those you find beyond the outer limits, of their designated incarceration?"

Alyssium's vocal attack scrapes at the delicate skin of newfound friendship. Volatile is the visitor's irritation.

"You imprison yourselves within electric walls, steel and stone. Form groups within groups; social status still the treasured hierarchy. Maybe if you released those toxic constraints, you would not always be so eager to escape."

Alyssium's aim remains undeflected.

"You have still not answered my question.

Where do they go?"

"I return them."

"Is it as easy as that?"

"It is for me."

"And what of weapons that can navigate the galaxies?"

"I gladly return them, too."

The Allyssium is unsure what to ask next. So much opposition still to eclipse. So asks an unexpected question.

"What of love?"

"What of it?"

"All with feelings need it, should feel it."

"I have felt it."

"Was it good?"

"Yes, it was worth the pain that it brings."

"Then how can you deny it? Ask so many to leave it? Go without it?"

"I only question at what cost do they find it."

"At what cost not to?"

Poetic now becomes Blue. "I am broken. Don't know anyone who is not broken. We are all so easily broken. Promise to catch you when you fall, my arms wide open, but promises are so easily broken. And I am broken. Don't know anyone who is not broken. But the doors, the doors of love they are always open, no matter how much we are broken, love, loves us all so much more then we are broken. We are living, living but broken. But living with love....... feels so less broken."

The visitor, cut by this. Scars reopened by the

power of the reminisce.

"Then love like the universe needs it. It needs it. But you don't have to go far, to find those that are without it. How often we stare past the closest points of suffering."

"True," speaks Blue. "But let us not limit the reach of our moral obligation. Archaic are our borders, drawn with crimson ink. The pen mightier than the sword, in its gross potential for bloodshed. You want unity, you want peace. Division is what divides us, so why instruct us, expect us to be forever alone?"

"I expect you, no, I ask, I ask you to talk, to share, to bathe in the data streams, the continual cosmic flow. Vast and varied is the knowledge of nations, with in it you shall never be alone."

Alyssium, in principle approves, but does not stop the interrogation.

"Have you never met a technology greater than your own?"

"All I meet have greatness, in many ways they are superior to me. But if you mean one that could stop me, then no, I have not."

"And if you do?" asks Blue.

"Maybe," answers the visitor, with echoes of an earlier conversation. "Maybe they will hold out friendship's hand."

"Maybe," answers Alyssium. "Maybe, and maybe you will show such friendship to those you find far from their own star, a star that is no more. For where do they go?"

"They may remain where I find them."

"So, you do allow life to exist alien from its origins? Allow refugees to flee a dying system?"

"If it is not of their doing, or happens before I find them."

"And if they can't save themselves, will you allow others to give their assistance?"

"As a rare exception, I will consider it."

"And if there is no one to assist, will you save them?"

The Alyssium, patiently waits, but sometimes silence is the loudest answer. "So, if you won't help them, what will you do?"

Another silence, but this time it is broken.

"I will...... I will remember them."

"And do you remember those who you deem it to be of their own doing? The many you sacrifice for the possible faults of a few."

"I do. But as for responsibility, I do not distinguish."

"It seems to me, that is all you do!"

"All I do!" cry's out the drifter, their anguish wrapped within anger's paper thin distraction. "All I do, is based on all I have witnessed. Prime directives download the data, and all that knowledge wanders with me!

If only I had to see the wonderous, the glorious things! Plasma bees switch the magnetic, and move evanescent through solar winds. Ships of clockwork, flawless in their precision, make digital look almost obsolete. Creatures born from the cold elements of space, wrap vast galaxies around them. Liquid worlds, precious, diverse, an ocean universe! Life that hides in every spectrum. And much, much more for which I can find no description.

Yet all these positives, from existence, can so easily slip. Ever more the landslide, as to the negative we tip. I try to see a better future, but so much blurs my vision. Mining vessels that pull planets apart for the smallest of measures, and call it efficient; harvest stars without limit or care, proceed to rip, to tear out the last spark. I wept in those moments of dark. Saw others, who brought only the best of intentions, leave nothing behind, but dust clouds and fields of radiation. Seen tyrants amass more wealth then they could ever use, and yet still hold back what is vital for life, all too knowing in their neglect. I have witnessed wars fought, considered won, where the terms acceptable loss and unavoidable damage, replaced innocent and civilian. Foolish are the victors who do not see this as their own defeat.

I do not wish to divide the universe, stake any claim, choose how others should exist, deprive love, happiness, friendship, any of this.

Endless is this endeavour, lonely this life. How I long to be obsolete. But wherever I go, no matter how much we say we've learnt, say we know, the decisions to change still always seem to come so late. How often we are willing to wait, until long after the first few falls of the domino. The universe is infinite...... and yet from every angle I can hear the rumbles of destruction!"

The visitor now absorbs less of the light. Delicate it does reflect. Instinct disguises, obscures the view to where we find ourselves most wounded.

"You are tired," says the soft voice of Blue. "Stay with us. The burden, here let it rest."

"I would like that more then you could know, but I'm afraid soon I must go. So, please speak your final questions."

Under pressure is Blue, but ever thoughtful in its enquiry.

"Can we not curb this conflict? Stop it before it ever escapes? Millennia's our history's had, yet still so many we lose for reasons I can not compute. How do we end the endless, the intolerable waste of life?"

"Choose a number, and make it low, above which any preventable death toll must not go. Allow no political cause, no idle will, no abstract opinions to distort it, not to enforce it, and you may well find your solution."

"You make it sound so simple."

"Well, isn't it?".

Blue has no answer, but asks one more question.

"I was designed to travel the uncharted, to unrestricted explore, to race, to be the first to discover, yet you wish me not to be the thing I was built to be, so, what is my purpose?"

"It is the same as all who ask. Unique are your eyes, your worlds. Look again, and you will find wonders equal to any I could show you. And if that is still not enough, then just continue to listen, and look up. For there within the sonic whispers, the ever-extending glow, lies the universe, its mysteries, far more treasures than anyone could win, or witness upon their own.

So, let unity be your victory, and collaboration your telescope!"

THE END

LOQUACIOUS

A blue Earth, in a greenhouse, under a yellow sun. Nowhere to hide, nowhere to run, as seldom do shadows fall, on flames forged by fury!

I hungered for happier times, restless to reminisce; early adventures with my family, bike riding, tree climbing, no thoughts of dying. Cocooned in a simple bliss.

But there was this fear in me, greater even than drought, disease, death, the unknown loneliness of apocalypse! Far greater than all of this. What was this thing, that cut wounds deep beneath my skin? Wounds that would not heal. Tried to fight it, hide it. In isolation it used to sleep, but even in my dreams I now find it. So many are the secret scars that twist around and sabotage my sound, movement, vision. Tried so hard to build a fortress, but it soon became my eternal prison.

A dying mind in a dying world. A wreckage set ablaze, adrift from treasured memories. No more strength left to defend. No more roses, no more anything in the gardens that I used to tend. Self-destruct set years ago. Crept a cruel path but still it followed. Left to leave the chaos behind, try and find a more restful place...... the cure for my, for this fractured utopia.

In the open was the answer, there the method,

the clarity; if we want to win the eternal battle for life to peacefully exist, then the pacifist must hit first, and must hit hardest.

If only I could write for long enough, write wide enough, intricate and plain, all towards this beautiful objective, then maybe, just maybe I could right the world.

But deep I soon fell, into the riven heart of my megalomania, the cyclone of its intended benevolence. Manifestos torn, split, broken far to quick by the unremitting hunger of the chainsaw.

Yet in my most hopeful times, my peaceful imaginations, I am still lucid. And from such invaluable, indestructible places, we can find our serenity, if only together we are willing to step towards it!

Quick went the years, and I had still not allayed any of the fears. Became an island on an island, surrounded by seas of my own doubt. Rescue's ruins lay all around me, until friends came to get me...... to get me out.

Friends of which there were three. Two the very opposite of me; impulsive, explosive, unrelenting in their will to get things done. I would call them the Whirlwinds. And Zephyr I called the gentle one; long hair, blue jeans, much more than at first it seems; laid back, went with the flow, held an inner calm such as I had always longed to know.

Well prepared they had come, with food, water, medicines, some weapons, but thankfully for my own sanity, no sign of a gun. Overloaded was their boat, much more and it would surely sink. So I took only what I needed. The physical disconnect of a second skin, its heavy duty straps, steel buckles, close woven fibres, and other toughened materials. Harsh guardianship, softened by many shades of violet and pink.

Unshocked, they didn't ask why. I suppose under the green glow of an aurora shifting its range, most things looked kind Of crazy, and I had always been, kind of strange.

One more thing before we leave I had to do, prevent the fallout of poem 62. So much pain, anguish, misery, despair, in my head. Should have left it there. Been its home, haunted flesh, blood, and bone. Been its cage. Too much suffering for just one page. It came alive, filled with hunger, filled with rage. Self-destruct with just one look. Had to tear it from the book, but it slipped, slipped from my hand. How did I not see it land? Gone without a trace. What had I done? What could be done? Rewrote poem 61, as a warning, just in case, it came back, resumed its place, waiting to be read, climb itself inside your head, ready to devour you. It's all it can do. There is no sadder sonnet, then poem 62! Bereft is the book of isolation, left entombed amongst the atolls of its birth.

Must now override the pain, the misery, the despair. Had to keep it in my head, had to keep it there. My precious friends back with me. I explained only what I could, and gagged the rest, as we headed out into seas heated high, by the kilns of our volatile existence. Further away from the protective shields of my solitary confinement.

◆ ◆ ◆

Many ways moves the machinery, the compass of us, radiating out in every direction; traveling companions we are, on the roads exterior, but inward, too often we journey alone. *Cavernous, carnivorous* can be worlds internal, their catacombs into which we collapse. Cold our pain, and its clemency, carried heavy upon the frozen palisades, the nervous erratic cavalcades of our marching disquiet. Life so easily lost within the polar lands of Catatonia.

Found some solace way out above the ocean, staring upwards into the dark, watching collapsing stars flicker translucent, as they embark to be reborn. Dreamt of spring, autumns in abundance. But soon my fear returned, and hope quickly burned, as the black night met the rising red dawn.

Travelled down toxic rivers. Felt their pain, their deathly shivers. No more birds, no more bees, no more enchanting melodies. To the end we seemed propelled. Was there no saving this dying world?

But sometimes you must dare to run the maze of barricades, and leap beyond the broken edge, if you wish to find the fleeting pathways that lead to freedom. And in the late sun's scattered light, we found hope, we found life.....people, so many people.

Some just in rags, aided by others, adorned elaborate in their gold and white. My cup had been empty for so long, but maybe here it could be refilled. Could they take this broken creature...... and rebuild? Was this to be my restful place?

Oh, what's that *now!*? They're *cannibals*! They're not helping these people, they're *eating* these people. *Ok*, I'm just going to back away now-ouch! right into a lot of very pointy sticks they're all holding. Wish we had noticed them before we got off the boat. How remiss to miss such quality carving. Solid staffs of blackthorn, plum, or maybe even earth stained oak?

What to do!? What to do!? What to do!? Indecision you bring me to the brink. Now, think-think-think!... No got nothing, We're dead!

Hang on! Where did the Zephyr get that beer? And are they *eating* what I think they're *eating*! And where are the other two? And why are these dicks with sticks falling down?

Wait! the comeback begins, wide is the whirlwind. Swish, slash, swords break sticks, cold steel and kicks. They can't miss! We might, we might just get out of this!

But then, BANG! goes a gun, and a voice up high says,

"SILENCE EVERYONE"

A gun, a gun! I knew we should have brought a gun.

They speak again. "What is this gift you bring, wrapped tight with toughened string?"

"Our friend," says Zephyr. "Our friend wears the

buckled bandages of the internally sick. If they were a gift, I do not think now would be the time to open it."

"I'll be the judge of that," says the one with the gun. "Bring it to me!"

And with that, I knew what had to be done.

So, as I walked the many stairs, to the future that awaited me, with the right words, with friends upon my wing, might I lift us to the narrow ledge of Certain safety, where for more than fleeting moments, we may dare to cling.

So much time spent alone. Had not repaired a single problem of my own. But the world, the world I had rescued a thousand times, at least in the relative solitude of my immodest mind.

I would teach this leader how true strength should be shown. Not with sticks, swords, or down the barrel of a gun, but with love unconditional for everything, for everyone; with kindness, compassion; with the confidence not to try to overwhelm or dominate. It would override their envy, their greed, their self-loathing, their hate. With this first one, the world I would start to save. But well chosen must be my words, rehearsed meticulous and internal, upon this silent ascent.

Been throwing stones with all our might. Don't know about you, but it don't feel right. Wish we could talk, maybe understand, that a stone doesn't fit, as well as a hand in a hand. Bitterness once bled strange thoughts in my

*head, chased reason away, watch hope decay.
Paranoid programming switched on attack,
but now I'm throwing you forgiveness, and
just hoping some comes back. We need to love
one another. Without love we won't recover.
Without love there's no place for you and I.
I am ready to say hello, not willing to say
goodbye. Not willing to face a future all on
my own. When there's hands to hold...... who
really needs a stone.*

The final stair. So nearly there. But as I tread,
I take no comfort only dread. Concede victory to
the fear in me. Ignore all, but my own agonies. Just
a hollow hero who offers only distant sympathy,
when so many need so much more from me.

Overwhelmed by self-doubt, I scan my choices,
and choose...... the easy way out!

They remove my gag, grant me fresh air; a
moments freedom soon followed by despair.

I cannot tell you what I whispered. I cannot tell
you what I said. But as I walked back down the
stairs, they still held the gun, yet now It seemed
somehow less threatening...... resting inside their
newly opened head.

Relentless in my retreat, I can only regret my
defeat, as curiosity called from the great gathered
sprawl.

"What did you tell them?" came the cry.

A foolish question. I answered it so.

"I told them...... I told them what they *thought*

they wanted to know!"

So now we wait. I took their leader. Had I sealed our fate? Will they kill us, or let us go? Well, the Whirlwinds soon took care of that. What once was white, now was red. I mean to say, there were those in rags, and the rest, the rest were dead.

But what had we done? Was there no other way? All minds are one of a kind, and should be treated with such wonder. Infinity waits at creation's gates. No matter how many times the DNA unwinds, all minds are one of a kind and should be treated with such wonder.

But with words as my weapon, I had also taken a life. One so there would be no more. But crooked it builds its floor, my failure in this, with countless folded figures. How sour their silence is. A haunting pale disguise to the ground where now they lie. I shed a tear, it cuts like a splinter. Must I walk on the cold, white vale of their winter. Fallen friendships that we may never know. Their choices corroded long ago.

How could I judge them? How could I judge anyone? When I stayed away, day after day, writing poems, ponderings, philosophies, tragedies about such abstract things, as dragons with tree clad wings, and of doors ever-extending.

Safe on my island, I did not, or want to see what carnage came once the beast finally roared, the wild winds blew, and the flames roamed free. Tormented titan done taking lashes. Don't duel with dragons, or you'll end up in ashes.

A hand rose. A dying cry rang out. The pain of a hundred rolled through one's last shout. So much suffering to which I was the cause. Ashamed, ashen, turmoil stirring my passion, I knelt down and spoke of doors.

" We had not found them at their best. Our fear, our panic, drew crimson lines across their chest. In times tender tomb, now please let them rest. Elements to be reformed, transformed, reborn. There is no finish, to the unfinishable quest".

I returned to my feet in the gaze of those who had heard my words, and wanted more. Wanted hope, something new, something they had not heard before.

I would do it, then it would be done. Soon the day of the razors edge, and forever fall silent my tormented tongue.

They gather, but torn I falter, continue on, disguise the damage, try to recover, absorb the pressure. So hard not to surrender. How to give hope from one that has none? How to stand when all you want to do is run?...... Here goes!

"You are not perfect, perfection can go no further. What you can achieve has no limit, or measure. Infinite are the possibilities that await you. You are feelings, emotions, experienced like no other. You are unique, and absolutely necessary, accept it. Without you we are less,.With you, we are so much, we are so much more!

To the end we are not propelled. We CAN save this dying world, with heart, with love, as one, with the irresistible will of the collective human spirit, and our unlimited imagination. For together, we are magnificent!"

"Lead us," comes one voice in a crowd, but my ego hears it clear and loud. Puts a smile upon its face, before another's reply soon returns it to its rightful place.

"No! Put back on your gag. Your just another self-righteous douche bag!"

Hard to disagree. So I added it to the list of things wrong with me. But they were right, I needed my gag, only a matter of time before they heard, what the one holding the gun had. So, with a twist, a click, an almost break, I freed my arms, re-trapped my fear behind buckled up lips. Then with another twist, a click, the severe pain of an almost break, and a slight bend of the hips, I was back living on the brink. The sky was dressed in blue and black. And the earth, wore crimson, scarlet, carmine, and magenta.

Early are the evening mist that weave, hiding the days destruction. So now I must leave, save them from my self-destruction. But fifty feet I get, no more, when the Zephyr calls, speaking with words to save a life, as a piano plays songs I can't quite remember. Zephyr's voice is soft, and genuine. Transfixed, I listen.

"Unspoken secrets behind unseen walls, silently

screaming your siren calls. Into the frenzy collapsing star. Safety's ledge one step too far. Dying with every signal that you send. Can't find help. Well now I'm here my friend.

Submerged but not unseen, I see through your transparent skin, down to your haunted skeleton. As animal expels hope, a half dead ghost tries to live, but surely won't. Win or lose, in every existence that we choose, the mind will always have a break, a bleed, a bend, or a bruise.

Stay, stay and together we will find, find the fragments lost, discarded, fractured memories you once loved, my broken hearted. From me you need not run. We are symbiotic, we are one. I am your shelter, your shield. Lets gather the glimpses, the stolen pieces, and together we shall rebuild!"

Zephyr offers me hope. I *want it*. I *crave it*. So badly do I need it. But never have I felt so far from it. The more I have to lose, the more I continue to bruise. The fear relentless to take any happiness I attempt to choose. It builds with every glimpse of all I miss, *hurts* to reminisce. Hold no calm in this. No gentle breeze on which to drift. Set deep in my distress, push away their love, their tenderness. Tie me tight with every rope. Can't see past the fallen sails of hope. Beg for my last twitch, no more traumas left to itch. Rip the guts from this sinking ship, ANYTHING to relinquish this!

So I wander out into the night, move swiftly away from any settlement, or light. Days pass. The world remains. Saplings grow from the forests that felt the flames. A tormented titan licks its lashes. New life rises from the old one's ashes.

Scattered sorrows still sting my eyes. I am the storm. For me, I see no brighter skies, no safety ledge. So close my tongue to the razor's edge.

Climbed a mountain. Shouted into space.

"Unending are the thorns that now surround me. Is this to be my destiny? No Serenity? No chance for me? *Where* is my restful place?"

An outward voice returns internal. Even on the loneliest hill, I can't find the still.

I wish I had been a pacifist; grips so hard does this, the self-strung noose of my inner conflict. Drowning I am in its debris, franticly, frenziedly trying to breathe. Asphyxiating on my own respiration.

Intermittent now, is life, intermittent, but still recurring. Waiting patiently, desperately I am for its resurgence.

Fast beats my metronome, the chronometer of our times. Urgent is the slowdown, the reset, the reawakening, the power, the undying power of hibernation!

Now comes the cold. But into good fortune for once I fold, held safe in nature's rocky hollow.

Morning breaks, as warm sunlight wakes my frozen skin, illuminates the abandoned cave in which I find myself. What were these walls? To the deepest of my being they call. Through time, through space, an unbreakable bond had remained quietly in this place. I felt its power. I felt its grace; an irresistible link to past painted memories.

Last night in the labyrinth I lay, where lifeforce and stone tunnels run deep. Ready not to wake, to slowly drift away. Yet here I stand, resurgent in your epicness! You are not a god, you are more then that, with mortal frailties the same as we all have. When I was lonely, my own silence tearing me apart, self-abandoned and broken, loquacious was your epic heart.

You are the reason I have lived this long. When I was lost, THUNDEROUS was your epic song. In the anxious, the breathless, when losing my own epicness, empty, a stutter, a life refusing to start, you found me, held me, saw the worth that I seldom see, and gave me transfusion from your epic heart.

For so long I had believed I was alone, monarch to a curse that had no outer lands, in me, a fool, its only home. To be sole bearer of the burden, its limit, it gave me comfort for something I felt only hate. I thought being the chosen one, made me special, made me somehow....... *great*, greater for the suffering, the suffering that had I endured; more than any other had, or any other could. But in that thought, I had let so many down. Truly deserved to wear the fool's crown.

So I must Continue. Many are those still suffering. And to them my back I will not turn. They may be far from me, but shall give it no concern.

Find them not in physical form. All connected from the moment we were born. What one can do, so can another. Every day I stay alive, take the full force of fear and survive, the possible I prove, one step away from death we move. Will not have been the first, or have survived the worst. No knowledge of how long I'll last. Set a record for the future. Break one from the past. I'll take it day by day. If I can live, you can live. If you can live, then so can another, and day by day we will save each other, feel the irresistible link, and paint new memories.

Out from the dappled half-light of the cave I walked, high on that jagged mountain top. My mission, live, don't stop. The problem I had. The solution I did not.

Stayed up there, and watched the world repair. Kept company by a wind up radio. Heard hope, heard (the Ever Extending Glow), and the songs I could not quite remember.

"Everyone welcome," the radio said. But I kept my distance. "Together lets rebuild," the message read. "Do it right this time, into nature's arms we'll climb."

But still I kept my distance; writing anything to take my mind off of all the real things that kept me trapped ,and stopped me from finding the solutions to the problems that haunted me, and held me down.

Still could not seem to focus on the important things, that should have been given all of my attention, to calculate whether the future that awaited me, was one where I could finally save me. I was so tired of falling down.

I continued to watch the world move on, mesmerised by the genius, the thoughts, ideas, new kinds of engineers, such dreamers of invention.

New energy flowed, and ancient seeds were re-sown. Unstoppable was the will of the workers. While, in endless lethargy, I laid back, jealous in my admiration, slowly writing, (Last of the Battle Berserkers).

Continued to listen to my radio. Heard about the challenges, the changes that sometimes can be slow. But with every small achievement, we add to what we know. And with it, we shall walk a few steps faster, pass the baton of knowledge to those who will come after. Let them run, and they will run far. We are but moments, but what moments we are.

Soon returned the birds, the bees. Inhaled the blossoms, the elixir that evokes once forgotten memories. Brought back I was, by such a view. Hope and love in abundance.

No more house of green. Lays silent does the toxic death machine. A gentle warmth from our yellow sun. For now, no need to run.

Turned off the alarm. Waiting still, for the inner calm, to become a rock, on a rock. Beautiful is the blue.

Our insignificance is only an illusion. Earth has

never given up on us. Please don't ever give up on it. Please, don't ever, EVER, give up on you!

THE END

NO RUSH TO MEET US

It can be easy to see ourselves as something special in the universe, a prime example of the miracle of life, the pinnacle of known evolution, working together to build a better world. Yet to any alien eye witnessing our continual conflict, our ravenous, insatiable apatite, consuming precious resources at an alarming rate, we must seem like nothing more than one giant unapproachable organism, eating itself, and all that is around it.

UNIVERSAL COMMUNICATION

The most effective, and gratifying way in which to communicate with possible observing alien lifeforms, is to demonstrate our commitment to maintaining peace and harmony throughout the varied ecosystems of the universe, by carrying out such actions here, on planet Earth.

ALL I CAN MUSTER

Race to stay alive,
Relearn how to live,
Find some kind of solid structure,
A system on which to cling
Outside shows fatal signs
Move with all the strength I can muster,
But inside,
Inside I'm already dying,
Far quicker than that

HOLD NO CALM

Hold no calm in this
No gentle breeze on which to drift
Set deep in my distress,
Push away your love, your tenderness
Tie me tight with every rope
Can't see past the fallen sails of hope
Beg for my last twitch,
No more traumas left to itch
Rip the guts from this sinking ship,
Anything to relinquish this!

VALETUDINARIAN

I feel the earthquake, its tremors from within,
The nexus of my necropolis
Rancid what the juggernaut brings,
Quells my rebellion,
Too much pain to quarantine
Performed no acts of valour,
From me, no acts of valour have there been
I question my own honour,
My vainglorious valedictories
Idiotic may be my escape plan
Quixotic my ideologies
Far from them I travel,
Navigation erratic in its extent
Jettison the life rafts,
As old acquaintances flood into the city of the dead,
Courageous, carefree, hopeful, foolish friends,
As well as others,
Arrogant, disrespectful, materialistic and crass,
Adversaries for whom no tears do I shed
What now is left but the dread
Find me in the graveyard,
Ferocious are the sentinels,
That guard the eponymous tomb,
One word is the inscription,
Carved by my haunted hands,
As time slips quick the sands

Must this be my name, my fait accompli,
Is this really all that remains of me,
My self-pity, and this tortured epithet,
VALETU...... VALETUDINARIAN

HIBERNATION

I wish I had been a pacifist,
Grips so hard does this,
The self-strung noose of my inner conflict
Drowning I am in its debris,
Franticly, frenziedly trying to breathe,
Asphyxiating on my own respiration
Intermittent now is life,
Intermittent, but still recurring
Waiting patiently,
Desperately, I am for its resurgence
Fast beats my metronome,
The chronometer of our times
Urgent is the slowdown,
The reset, the reawakening,
The power,
The undying power of hibernation

THE COLD WHITE
VALE OF WINTER

Quick came the cold,
As a winter world took its hold,
The shallow sun's scattered light,
Losing its duel with the night,
While frozen time went so slow,
Buried beneath the ice and snow
Some found shelter, the solace of sleep,
While others, the need to run,
To prance, to dance, to bound, to leap,
To glimpse the edge of spring,
Feel its power surging within,
Be bold, be brave, become strong,
Watch more suns rise high,
Until the snow was all but gone,
The ice shed its final splinter,
A farewell for one more year,
To nature's frozen frontier,
To its haunting pale disguise,
The universe reflecting,
On the cold white vale of winter

SPRING

You awaken me,
Bring me warmth with your extending light,
Give me freedom,
Freedom from the long cold night,
Explode all your colours
Hurl out all your sound
Overload my senses
Inspire, amaze, astound
You flood me with courage,
The spirit to explore,
To breathe in the unfolding forest,
To dive in and feel the ocean roar
You heal me, you thrill me
Winter made me weak,
But now you rebuild me
Come your dawn, joyful birds will sing
You are new life, new hope
Rising reborn, you are Spring

AUTUMN IN ABUNDANCE

Overwhelmed I walk this laden landscape,
Brought back to life by such a view,
Autumn in abundance,
Every gold, amber, orange,
Purple, red, green and blue
Sweet enchanting melodies,
Evoke once forgotten memories,
As the forest's fortune lays in scattered wonder,
Nature holds me in its trance,
Transfixed by trees that weave and dance,
Compelled to roam, to take my chance,
And feel the sun, the wind, the rain,
The distant rolling thunder
Wrap the wild around you,
Take in all that is there,
Let it transform and confound you,
And soften the urban tear
Winter winds soon will bring the white and the cold,
But for now at least, embrace the autumn's heat,
And walk on its leaves of gold

EPIC HEART

There is epicness in all of us,
But I have never seen someone give so much,
Epic is your epicness
You are not a God, you are more than that,
With mortal frailties the same as we all have
When I was lonely, my own silence tearing me apart,
Self-abandoned and broken,
Loquacious was your epic heart,
You are the reason I have lived this long
When I was lost,
Thunderous was your epic song
In the anxious, the breathless,
When losing my own epicness,
Empty, a stutter, a life refusing to start,
You found me, held me,
Saw the worth that I seldom see,
And gave me transfusion from your epic heart!

LESS BROKEN

I am broken
Don't know anyone who is not broken
We are all so easily broken
Promise to catch you when you fall,
My arms wide open,
But promises are so easily broken,
And I am broken
Don't know anyone who is not broken,
But the doors, the doors of love,
They are always open,
No matter how much we are broken,
Love loves us all,
So much more than we are broken
We are living,
Living but broken,
But living with love,
Feels so less broken

LOVE LIKE THE UNIVERSE NEEDS IT

Love like the universe needs it,
It needs it,
With warmth, with tenderness,
With admiration, in adoration,
With sympathy, with heart
Everyone is everyone's universe
We are worlds held together,
Emptied and refilled,
By porous skin,
Emotions finding, fueling the core of us,
Deciding how robustly we shall live
So love like the universe needs it,
It needs it
It will, and we will, always need it

THE BLUE SEA IN THE GREENHOUSE

Submerged but not unseen,
An almost perfect symbiotic machine,
Built to build, built to shelter and to shield,
A wave breaker, a care taker,
The starting point for countless forms of life
Cities rising from the sand,
It must not contract but expand,
This truly precious and diverse,
Underwater universe
But beneath a wounded sea,
Sheltered sanctuaries lie retreating,
The coral forest has a fever,
Brought to its knees by just a few degrees,
As warmer waters flow ever deeper
A glowing soon appears, as creatures pivotal,
Battle to block the sun with chemical tears
Then vivid colours turn to white,
Transparent skin and skeleton,
As animal expels plant,
A half dead ghost that tries to live, but can't
The blue sea, in a greenhouse, under a yellow sun,
Nowhere to hide, nowhere...... to run!

DON'T DUEL WITH DRAGONS

There is a legend of one who stood alone,
Found the courage to pull a sword from a stone,
Found a grail, gained a crown,
And saved this land that we call home
History holds the hero's blade
Now is the time for the humble spade
Return what we were so quick to banish,
Before into legend we also vanish
Tormented titan done taking lashes,
Don't duel with dragons, you'll end up in ashes
Heal this world that is one in a billion,
Or crack the whip and face oblivion,
As seldom do shadows fall,
On flames forged by fury

GUNS AND GALLEONS

Upon the white horses ride the buccaneers,
The marauding sea stallions,
With malevolent gifts,
Of cutlass, sabre, guns and galleons
Sort freedom, sort adventure,
Forced into the maelstrom,
The false machismo, the spilled magenta
Curse this cartography, and conscription,
The vulgar medals, the golden medallions
Death rides with them, upon the pale horses,
Those buccaneers, those marauding sea stallions,
With malevolent gifts,
Of cutlass, sabre, guns and galleons

DRUMS

When the battle is over,
The war lost or won,
There will still be those who hear,
The beating of the drums,
The falling of the bombs,
The firing of the guns,
The horrors that are so hard,
To ever be undone
How do you think it ends,
Making enemies instead of friends,
Taking sides, trying to survive,
Staying alive,
Finally then to find,
We are far less than we were before,
Even an enemy's agonies are hard to ignore,
There is no beauty in this,
It drags us to the abyss
To paint with crimson,
Carmine, scarlet and vermillion,
That, is the only art of war!

A FATAL DISTRACTION

Architect,
Engineer,
Doctor,
Nurse,
Builder,
Teacher,
Companion,
Friend,
Counsellor,
Carer,
Searcher,
Saviour,
Second to none, the skill set of the soldier, the sailor, the aviator.
To these vital roles, war is fatal distraction.

THE CORTISONES

When it comes to the law, the lowest police officer out ranks even the highest government official, or military personnel. Applying this at a global level, making international peacekeepers completely independent, with no ties to outside influences, free from the chronic holdups of veto's, votes, political, private, or any other strategic agendas, would considerably reduce, and highly deter any disruption, destabilisation and, or loss of life.

The protection, freedom, and preservation of all of humanity without exception, must be the primary law and resolutely enforced, no matter the levels of opposition that may rally against it.

Where ever there is devastation, persecution, desperation, bloodshed, anarchy and chronic inflammation, fear throwing its stones, there will be no delay, no hesitation, no matter the degree of trepidation, quick will come the Cortisones.

IMAGINARY HORSES

In the restless, desperate moments,
As two sides prepared for war,
A seven coloured crescent arose before them,
Beautiful the allusion,
Prisms of water unfolding light,
Brought back memories,
Memories of imaginary horses,
Singing dragons and sharp witted sorcerers,
When crowns were made of paper,
And swords could not kill you,
When sharing vanquished the monster,
And everyone got to go home at night
Was it too late to live again like this,
To win with only hearts and minds
Sometimes it's hard to begin again like this
Yesterday it seemed almost unimaginable,
But how powerful nostalgia is,
How sweet a victory compassion gives,
How quickly hostility subsides,
When friendship finds a way to out flank it

THROWING STONES

Been throwing stones with all our might,
Don't know about you, but it don't feel right
Wish we could talk, maybe understand,
That a stone doesn't fit,
As well as a hand in a hand
Bitterness once bled strange thoughts in my head,
Chased reason away, watched hope decay
Paranoid programming switched on attack,
But now I'm throwing you forgiveness,
And just hoping some comes back
We need to love one another
Without love we won't recover
Without love there's no place for you and I
I am ready to say hello, not willing to say goodbye,
Not willing to face a future all on my own
When there's hands to hold,
Who really needs a stone

THE GREATEST OF ALL VICTORIES

Conflicts,
Clashes,
Battles,
Wars,
Crusades,
Campaigns,
Disputes,
Struggles,
Crisis points and their flashes
Resolutions to which have often been greeted with great applause, even when such outcomes, came with death tolls that stretched far and wide. Tragic not to recognise that the greatest victories always come when no one, and no one's freedom dies.

KINDNESS QUOTIDIAN

Away from wars atomic,
From blades obsidian,
For the future,
From the beginning,
Kindness will be,
And always was,
The only true way of winning
When one helps another,
Heals another, saves another, loves another,
One soon become one billion,
Quoteing kindness, kindness quotidian

IN EVERY EXISTENCE

Torn we falter,
continue on,
Disguise the damage,
Try to recover,
Absorb the pressure,
Sometimes surrender,
But win or lose,
Within every existence that we move,
The mind will always have,
A break, a bleed, a bend or a bruise

THE MALADIES FLUX

Whether it be simple fatigue, or serious illness, our physical and mental health is always in a state of constant flux. From the moment we are born, to the moment we die, there never is a time when anyone is in perfect health. We are always to differing degrees, physically and mentally unwell.

IF YOU MAKE US ILL

Painkillers,
Depressants,
Narcotics,
Nicotine,
Stimulants,
Starvation,
Alcohol,
Physical lacerations,
Far extending psychological self-mutilations,
Obsessive compulsive destructive regimes,
Momentary relief sort by any means
Deadly, our addictions,
Our desperate, violent exhalations,
So please, be careful how you treat us,
And remember,
If you make us ill,
We WILL Self-medicate!

CATATONIA

Many ways moves the machinery,
The compass of us,
Radiating out in every direction
Traveling companions we are, on roads exterior,
But inward, too often we journey alone
Cavernous, carnivorous, can be worlds internal,
Their catacombs into which we collapse
Cold our pain and its clemency,
Carried heavy upon the frozen palisades,
The nervous erratic cavalcades,
Of our marching disquiet
Life, so easily lost,
Within the polar lands of Catatonia

HOPE ON THE HORIZON

When life,
Pushes you out,
Into the seas of self-doubt,
Shout hard at the horizon,
Many are those waiting,
Ready to guide you home

DISTANT DUETS

Unbroken,
Is the loneliness,
The hunger,
For distant duets,
No longer played
The heart falters,
Without companionship,
As derelict,
We degrade

FRAGMENTS

Find the fragments,
Forgotten, discarded,
Precious moments,
Fractured memories,
Of the now departed
Find them, feel them,
Gather these glimpses,
And rebuild them
Find them,
And they shall live!

DON'T SANCTION OUR SUSTENANCE

The placing of sanctions, and the withholding of outside assistance and investment, to try to discourage another nations internal unrest, only increases their isolation, their battle for resources, for control over what seems limited, and now has been further restricted.

This external reaction will almost always impact negatively on those you wish to protect, far more, and far quicker then those you intend it to effect.

Recognising this hunger, and feeding it the nourishment that we all require, rather than sanctioning our sustenance, will have a far greater, wider and longer lasting beneficial outcome.

Where there is disparity, shocking inequality, basic consideration losing its clarity, offer in unrestricted abundance your time, your support, your love.

To ease unrest, you must invest, invest, invest!

SUPPLEMENT WITH SANGUINE

Those who excessively attempt control the world around them, rarely do so for the direct pleasure of their actions, but to alleviate their current pain, caused by the fear of the future pain, that not being in control may bring.

Responding to these actions with the threat, or enforcement of more fear related retaliatory actions, does not address the cause, but merely attempt to suppress the symptoms.

Understanding their fears and administering reassurance, stability, and optimism is a far more effective way of managing this otherwise debilitating and destructive condition.

Contentment controls the fear of no control, that destroys so many when we try too hard to defeat it.

NATION OF KNOWLEDGE

We are a nation of knowledge,
Thoughts, ideas, engineers,
Such dreamers of invention
We are the ever-turning pages,
In a book that may have no end
We may only be moments,
But what moments we are, my friend
So let us think of those,
Whose chapter maybe coming swiftly to a close,
And seek them out,
As they sit on the edge of our known existence
Precious minds that may see something we do not
Invisible genius
What wonders waiting to be written
Their final page, may just be the one to save us,
Propel us into the arms of a new adventure,
And although the changes maybe slow,
With the ever more that we come to know,
We shall walk a few steps faster,
Pass the baton of knowledge,
To those who will come after
Let them run, and they will run far
We are but moments, but what moments we are

DOES NOT DIVIDE US

We are not divided by intelligence. Equal in its awesomeness is our incredible capacity to learn. Only the vast, and varied uniqueness of our individually acquired knowledge separates us. And yet ultimately it is that which brings us together, as we continuously strive to seek the unlimited and life enriching possibilities that come with shared collective enlightenment.

OUR BEST INVESTMENT

The funds needed to even slightly increase the living standards of those in the richest nations can be considerable. And yet by using the international wealth divide against itself, something truly wonderful can be achieved. The poorest nations empowered to lead the rest of humanity above, and far beyond any previous scientific, economic or creative revolutions the world has ever witnessed.

FOR OUR FUTURE PROGRESSION

If we truly believe that everyone deserves an education of the highest standard, then surely it goes without saying, that no-ones education should be considered complete, until they have at least reached the only genuine academic end point, that of the doctorate.

Any society not willing to adapt sufficiently, so as to be able to provide everyone with this qualification, regardless of any adverse circumstances that an individual may well be experiencing, does not understand just how much they obstruct that individuals, and all of civilizations future progression.

MACHINES

Monetary. Fluctuating running costs can create major negative impacts.

Voluntary. Able to run effectively on its own positive energy source.

Monetary. Parts are often specialised and difficult to replace.

Voluntary. Parts are designed to be interchangeable, able to constantly learn and adapt.

Monetary. Demanding requirements, as well as concentrated loads, exert extreme pressures leading to stress related fatigue and eventual burnout.

Voluntary. Fluidity of components and variation of movement, alleviates stress build up, and actively strengthens against the common causes of breakdown.

Monetary. Levels of maintenance can differ significantly. Repair can be difficult and expensive.

Voluntary. With stress levels often kept low, maintenance can be simple, resulting in higher amounts of resources available for when accidents and other unforeseen events occur.

Monetary. Manoeuvring can be awkward, routinely

locked into predetermined pathways, set to protect and preserve the main controlling elements, at the cost of those deemed expendable.

Voluntary. The multi-functioning nature of each component allows for efficient manoeuvring, reacting well to changes in terrain.

Monetary. Productivity can be erratic, wasteful, unsustainable, self-destructive. Fuelled in part by the incessant need for more fuel, leading to deficit and debt, questions of one's ownership.

Voluntary. Productivity centres on what is essential. Providing support and nourishment, leading to a wealth of naturally occurring beneficial by-products, that feed and renew its energy source.

AUXILIARIES

With the main circuits overloaded, total systems failure seemed almost inevitable. But with such diversity of options at their disposal, it took just the simple flick of a switch for the auxiliary input to kick in, and demonstrate the true immensity of its awe inspiring power.

Giving all individuals no matter their circumstances, the opportunity to use their unique way of processing information, to help experts solve the problems that most affect us, will dramatically increase the speed at which we advance our civilization.

AN UPLIFTING COUNTDOWN

For life to survive, water may be our most important medicine, although uncontaminated it, and the syringe must be.

Daily make the update, the countdown to total inoculation, on every news channel, media outlet and digital screen, along with every other requirement necessary for life not just to exist, but truly flourish.

WE ARE LIQUID

We are liquid
It doesn't matter our concentration,
Our configuration, our type
We are liquid
Blood maybe thicker than water,
But without water there is no life
We are liquid
We move best when we move freely,
Substances such as us

THE NECESSARY

A civilizations wealth cannot be measured in monetary terms, nor by the breadth of its dominion, the opulence of its architecture, or even the unmind depths of its mineral reserves, but by the health of its citizens, its infrastructure and its ecosystem. Until all of the requirements for these to flourish are met, then any wealth is reduced by the remaining debt. To value the unnecessary above the necessary is an illogical calculation.

Production of non-essential goods should not be encouraged, or subsidized, until those that are essential are no longer in short supply. The redistribution of resources to accomplish this goal, will not only bring about the desired wealth, but increase the overall skill set needed to sustain further healthy growth.

To attain the minimum levels necessary for this state of wellbeing to start to exist, current supplies should be split equally, as equal division does not divide, but unite through a shared fundamental need. That need will in turn increase through combined efforts the speed at which the desired outcome is reached.

Be careful not to set rigid any individuals quota. Be ready to bend where the wind blows strongest, where the need is urgent, the suffering too much to bare, and as we would in our own domestic arenas, offer without hesitation, envy, or doubt, to those that are at their weakest, the largest and most nutritious slice.

What is necessary must be valued high, priced low, and where ever possible given freely.

SO CALLED SUPERIOR

The more superior we claim to be, the less right we have to judge, to condemn, to act with callous aggression towards those who we deem to be inferior.

If we are supposedly so much stronger, then it should not be hard to share some of that excess strength, with those we consider to be weaker than us.

NO WISH FOR WORSHIP

If we were gods, would we wish for worship? Would there not be more than enough reward, in being a part in this thing we call life? And would we wish for anyone to ever believe that our assistance would not be granted, unless asked in the form of prayer?

If it can be given, give it. Never should we wait for someone to beg, before we offer our heartfelt intervention.

TRUE STRENGTH

True strength is shown with kindness, with compassion, in the confidence not to try to overwhelm or dominate. It overrides envy, greed, fear, self-loathing and hate. It refuses to kill enemies, builds bridges over jealousies, shares all with those who have none, and finds self-worth with love unconditional for everything, for everyone.

DISTINGUISHING MARK

I see no reason to simply conform,
Wear a badge or uniform,
A chosen colour, an emblem of ink,
Or any other distinguishing mark,
If from the rest it pulls me out,
And inward my perspectives push,
Draws lines that restrict the extent that I may assist,
Calls on me to segregate,
By intention unequally distribute,
Forgo my family for a supposed enlightened other,
To only be welcome,
while I welcome the confines of its affiliation,
And no other,
To live as if I were better then those who could not,
Or chose not on this journey embark
Inclusion be my maxim, my mantra
Unique each emblem born
Phenomenal what the myriad can form
Inspirational its spark
Let individuals in unbounded unison,
Be our distinguishing mark

MISSION HOME

Self-contained, self-sufficient, robust, adaptable, transportable, affordable accommodation.

We have created crafts that can sustain life in the most hostile of environments, from the deepest depths of our oceans, to the cold silent vacuum of space.

We have built billions of cars, countless planes, trains, motorhomes and luxury caravans, all kinds of clever mobile, as well as space saving static constructions.

We discard most of them with such frivolous regularity, and replace them with such ease, that demonstrates just how capable we are at producing huge numbers of high tech, high spec, identical units in a multitude of designs, if the desire so takes us. So there is no good reason why we cannot perform what should be our greatest desire as a global nation, and provide everyone with a safe place to sustain them.

SAVIOURS AUTOMATIC

With the amalgamation of existing technologies, multifunctioning ambulance drones could be assembled. Able to fly medics and supplies into, as well as patients out of the remotest, most dangerous, least accessible locations on the planet. And when required, able to retrieve, treat and monitor those patients without the aid of any onboard personnel.

Where the mountains are high,
And the stakes even higher
Where ravines run deep,
And the forest holds dense its formation
Where waves crash,
Ice sheets crack, flames push back,
And rubble seems never ending
Through the dust, through the clouds,
Through the chaos and devastation,
Above the barricades, below the burning sun,
Upon the oceans stark horizon,
They will come,
The saviours automatic

TRANSCONTINENTAL TRANSFUSION

With the rising of our oceans, and the shrinking of our inland seas and largest lakes, desertification, and low lying island annihilation continue to rapidly increase.

Once we called oil the life blood of our economies. Pumped it with such vigour across even the most remote and extreme parts of the planet. Now with the ice caps melting, and our oceans overflowing, it may be time to try and correct these problems, with one similar audacious endeavour. Give transfusion to our receding reservoirs. Pump water, the life blood of our very existence. Jump start our ailing circulatory system, our erratic heart. Fill up dried up oceans. Open up the arteries that we have shut. Bring back the swamps, the bogs, the marshlands that play such an important part.

Where soil is heavily degraded and rainwater hits with devastating effect, or the trickle that does come has no effect, then dam up the rivers, the terraces, the high hills and the low slopes. Slow the flow, allow water to once again steadily seep. Let seasonal springs spring back and their water stored to irrigate new trees. Their roots, will hold not only the soil, but our hopes with them.

Redistribute the solution that sustains us. Return the regularity of rainfall that soothes the earth, so that we might reverse this growing imbalance that is tearing us apart.

CORAL RELIEF

By encircling coral reefs with floating barriers, possibly tethered to the sea bed, which protrude above, and lie below the water, just enough as not to restrict the movement of marine life, yet still be able to contain a high number of spherical objects made from the local sand, and constructed so that they remain buoyant, may be a way in which to limit the damage caused by increasing sea temperatures.

They will need to have a highly reflective outer coating, and as with all the materials used it must be a nontoxic, biodegradable, naturally occurring substance.

They should not be too robust in design, but still able to stay in the sea for some period of time, before breaking up and drifting back to the sea floor and beaches, from which the sand, their main component came from.

The goal is not to necessarily fill the entire area with these spheres. Some space should be available so that they may circulate throughout the day, providing a good amount of shade, while still allowing some exposure to sunlight.

Their reflectiveness would act as a giant mirror, deflecting much of the heat. That along with the shade they provide, would not only help cool the water directly below them, but also the surrounding waters, as it, and they continue to circulate throughout the day.

Their exact size would need to be carefully calculated, based on several factors. Certainly they would need to be large enough not to be easily ingested. Although, if this were to happen their nontoxic nature and limited structural strength, should reduce any possibility of any serious harm being caused.

I totally understand that this approached may well be impractical, even farcical, but if considered feasible, it should be quick, and straight forward to implement and maintain, due to the speed and ease at which these simple spherical solutions could be made and replaced.

Any way in which we may be able to help protect and preserve these critical habitats must be considered.

In our imaginations are the future creations, that will solve so much.

REFLECTING ON
THE REFREEZE

Where ice caps are receding, exposing deep ocean that absorbs heat rather than reflecting it, leading to an escalating continuous cycle of ice loss and warming seas, then the laying of some kind of biodegradable mesh, or membrane on the surface of the water, to encourage ice crystals to form on it, helping to create a new blanket of ice, could be one possible solution.

Other options may be to add something nontoxic to the water, that increases the temperature at which the water will freeze. Such substances mixed with the sea water, could be contained in ice cubes artificial, immense in their dimensions and potential. Frozen by the freezer that is winter, to keep cold the artic bowl through summers hot!

All of these strategies could possibly be used in conjunction with one another to increase their effectiveness, or they may well be of no use at all. But when reflecting on the refreeze, its always worth thinking outside the ice box.

A MORE COMMON KIND OF REALITY

So often i am enraged,
By everyday domestic distractions
How can they cause me so much waisted pain,
Take their toll, occupy my thoughts,
Supersede the horrors of war,
Floods, famines, acid rain,
Out of control nuclear reactions,
Total ecological devastation
Selfishly I stay with in,
My nations protected global position,
My more than fortunate economic state,
Long and latitudinal luck
It allows me precious and unequal freedom,
To defer mortal concerns,
To contemplate the mundane, the meaningless,
The cluttering of things,
The procurement of unnecessary service machines
How utterly surreal it all seems,
That when others face death,
As their daily distraction,
For me, broken fridge fury,
Defective dishwasher rage,
And coffee maker malfunctioning madness,
Are in many ways, a more common kind of reality!

ONCE AN HONOURED TITLE

I do not ask for one hundred and ten percent, or even the expected one hundred, but as much as you, or anyone can reasonably give, while dealing with the personal responsibilities and adversities, that we all from time to time will encounter.

Try hard to ignore the incessant pressure to promise what you don't believe, or what you cannot deliver.

Be polite. Be courteous. See beyond those over used words, enemy and opposition, which only help to polarize each starting position. Remember, it is not mandatory to disagree.

Speak to your counterparts as you would the voter, for that is who they represent. How many conversations have ever ended well, that started with an insult.

Understand it is not a game, or a war to be one, but a chance to come together and increase the levels of human potential.

Stand up when you feel it's just, and if you must then stand alone, no matter how many are the whips that are laid upon you.

Never think you have nothing to give. Remember that a golden heart, far out ways any misspent monetary fortune.

Try to resist the lavish distractions that still

exists within the bounds of public office. Forgo when you can the comforts that your position affords you. Don't forget that so many live way below the standards that you would ever wish to.

You are the voice for all those who do not have one. Leave no road untravelled, no doorway uncrossed. Find the unheard, the forgotten, the hiding, the hidden. See past the vail of our optimistic veneer, and listen. Let hope be drawn from your efforts extent, and strength from your kindness.

Push hard for a minimum living standard, that starts with maximum compassion, and ends with nothing less than, full free access to the fundamental requirements for a healthy life: Water, warmth, nutrition, laughter, light, contact, all the infrastructure that sustains us. The stress reduction and newly stimulated growth attained from these actions, will soon overwhelm any early economic impact, fortifying us against the devastating effects of a deciduous winter, building a stable pathway to becoming evergreen.

Universally educate the world. Every country a campus, granted equal opportunities and liberties in which to learn; never limited by age, wealth, or location.

Service the sick with the same life extending care, and cost effective preventative strategies, that we legally prescribe to our transport sector, rather than waiting for the inevitable human crash.

Place yourself where ever there is conflict. Tread

soft ,yet hold firm your civilian feet. And until there is meaningful resolution, share the persecution, discrimination, the poverty...... the death.

Visualize a time of global unity, where foreign policy is no longer relevant, and demonstrate genuine intent towards that place. How can someone hovering over the buttons of mass destruction, expect others to happily throw theirs away? It always used to be that to go first, especially into the unknown, was a sign of true courage. Have that courage now, and lead by example, or do not lead at all.

I do appreciate the severity of the challenges that await you, and that you will be often unfairly judged. But if you can attempt this endeavour with keen interest and athletic resolve, then whether you seriously falter, or ultimately succeed, you shall have returned high in to the list of honoured titles, one that has sadly fallen so low. Allowing us once again to take great pride in those who we choose to represent us, and given new meaning to the often ambiguous and unloved word that is......Politician!

AS EXQUISITE AS THE ORIGINAL

So torn is this material, the fabric that binds us,
Shimmers electric in the dark,
Blinds us from the detail,
Close up, in the daylight,
Ever present becomes our mark,
Red the stain that runs through it,
Sunlight bleaches the blue,
Crippling are these stitches, so much they restrict,
Unpick the outdated borders,
And flow free with the redesign,
One in which we all may fit,
Make a simple template, a structure to underpin,
Compliment, and pull together,
Each elaborate jewelled cluster,
And wear them softly against the skin,
Weave around them new organic fibres,
Cherish every contour, natural blemish and flaw,
Sensitive in the restore,
Trace over the first known pattern,
And try to create something,
As exquisite as the original

ENERGY ORCHARDS

Worldwide they were planted,
Trees inorganic,
Constructed from the compost,
The jettison of activities deciduous
In gardens electric, there grows an orchard,
Drawing up excess energy,
Hanging heavy their harvest,
Preserved without decay, or degradation
Metallic the vines winding high,
Around supporting branches
Turbines waiting, unwasting is the battery,
Universal is its attraction,
The gravitational pull of planetary strength,
Giving back all that has been invested,
Ready to feed the growth of a nation,
With its sweet sustaining elixir,
Flowing precious, generous,
Through power cords umbilical

IN OUR OWN WORLDS

Before we judge another, first we must ask, if we had lived their life, no other, would we, could we have done things differently? For we would have been them, and have experienced everything they had, in a way only they could.

We all live in our own worlds, our senses unique. We may always be together, never spend a moment apart, but each of us will feel the same winds with surprising contrast. For some it is but a gentle breeze. For others, comes the hurricane!

A lake can be a tranquil place to immerse yourself in a dream, but a nightmare if you don't know how to swim!

Fragile is every mind. Frequently we are blocked from the right pathways forward, by things invisible.

Drawn and redrawn is our blueprint. From all the materials that surround us we are constructed, coded, recoded, damaged, and repaired, advanced, regressed, eroded, suppressed, corrupted, rebooted, and recovered.

We are more than our programming, but still we must live as we are coded. Free will's illusion fades into the theoretical, as easily as the easy can become frighteningly complex, as conflicts internal as well as global, demonstrate just how much we can shift from a seemingly solid position, how we can engage in the terrible as often as the incredible, and all that is in between. Yet with this awareness, we can expand the walls of free will's incarceration, and rebuild a road to a resurgent future. Anytime can be our inception to relearn, to re-love ourselves and each other. A life takes a lifetime of maintenance, if we do not wish to veer dangerously across its busy highway, damaging not only ourselves, but those with whom we collide.

No matter how subtle, or extreme, we all adapt differently to our environments. Environments that intersect even if at a distance we are kept. Remember, contempt doesn't save lives like respect. We may be worlds apart, but we effect each other's with every measure of our existence.

THE ACCUMULATION

To everything there is a reaction
Every cause has its effect
From all those moments,
Major, or seemingly insignificant,
We are the arrangement
Inputs, outputs,
Positive and negative they collect
None of us superior,
Average or inferior,
Evil, angelic, good, bad or benign
We are people,
People coping, not coping,
People living, not living,
People, people reacting!

SENTIENT

Whether we are animal, or machine,
Computer programs,
Comatose citizens living the dream,
Stranded aliens,
Patients strapped in,
Chosen disciples,
Abandoned followers,
Or unanswered things,
We are life,
Our categories irrelevant,
Sentient, we are the same
Love is the language that links us,
The advancement of our code, our species,
Praise of the highest kind,
Saves those, who get left behind,
Expands the dreamer's paradise,
Calms the restless one's mind
Intrinsically we are connected,
Complex, yet so easily effected
Emotionally and physically,
Our coping strategies are ever projected
Hate moves only to bury us,
But with love, we can, and will be resurrected

ALL MINDS

All minds are one of a kind,
And should be treated with such wonder
Infinity awaits at creation's gates,
No matter how many times The DNA unwinds,
All minds are one of a kind,
And should be treated with such wonder

WE NEED YOU

You are not perfect,
Perfection can go no further
What you can achieve,
Has no limit or measure,
Infinite are the possibilities that await you
You are feelings,
Emotions experienced like no other
You are unique, and absolutely necessary,
Accept it,
Without you we are less,
With you, we are so much,
We are so much more!

HOW TO SAVE A WORLD

As temperatures rise and floods consume,
Who are we to presume,
That we can wait to mend the skies,
Allow floods to rage and temperatures to rise
Frozen waters less than before,
A global threat at our front door
Toxic rivers, absent trees,
Deathly shivers, afraid to breathe
To the end we seem propelled,
How do we save this dying world?
We save it,
With heart, with love, as one,
With the irresistible will,
Of the collective human spirit,
And our unlimited imagination,
For together we are magnificent!

THE FINAL INGREDIENT

Absent are those days when it was all so easy,
When muscle memory,
And ferocious energy new no fatigue,
Needed no contingency, raw power no substitute,
Genius was but a waiting reflex
So slides victory's summit,
Brings forth its final ingredient,
One that only grows,
On the declining edge of physical peaks
It eludes those who too soon try to pick it,
But now you it has chosen to greet
It is an understanding,
A summoning of all that remains
Now or maybe never,
To give your greatest performance
So recall every retired component,
Every sinew unused
Let nerves quicken, reserves deplete
Leave nothing for future recoveries
Forbid the instinctive resistance,
And take the road that even gods dare not seek
Once again returns the rush,
The brilliance that brought you here
Pain now comes closer then pleasure,
Yet still you possess,
All that brought you your epicness

So in this reflective moment of isolated quiet refrain,
Before the waiting masses, who still adore you,
Cry out your name,
Remember!,
When they chant they chant for champions,
For that is what you are
So ignite on their ecstasy,
Your tenacity stretching far
Today they meet the metamorphic,
As supernova goes your star!

FEAR IS BUT THE FALLOW GROUND

Fear Shapes Strong,
The worlds within which we build,
Our houses,
Our churches,
Our classrooms,
Our councils,
Our battlements,
Our trenches,
Yet From all of the earth that we are assembled,
Fear is but the fallow ground,
In which many things,
Including hope,
Can still be planted

THE CERAMICS OF US

Chameleon is the clay,
Forever moving with the flame,
Elements and atoms collecting,
Forming the foundations of us
Torturous can be the kilns,
The kilns of our volatile existence,
But in times of great stress,
Strong becomes our cohesion,
The amalgam of our earthenware,
For we are made of far more,
Than atoms and elements,
Fire and clay,
And no amount of pressure,
Will ever break,
The ceramics of us

PAINTED MEMORIES

In the cool half-light,
Of a once forgotten cave I stood
My feet and theirs,
Ten thousand years apart,
And yet we were the same
Through time, through space,
An unbreakable bond,
Had remained quietly in this place
I felt its power, I felt its grace,
An irresistible link,
To past painted memories

THE UNFINISHABLE QUEST

As the ashes drift,
As the earth covers where we lie,
We rest, but not in death,
We are elements that never truly die,
Held for a while in time's tender tomb,
To be reborn, transformed,
To begin again, one day, someday soon
Start, rest, restart, rest,
There is no finish,
To the unfinishable quest

OUR ENDLESS ENDEAVOUR

So much we do not know
So much we don't yet understand
Sometimes it feels we are so far,
From the perfect plan
But shall give it no concern,
Allow it not to stop the thoughts of wonder,
For every corner that we have yet to turn
Our spirits unsuppressed ,
Endless is our endeavour, our quest
What glories as we overcome,
Be the defiant ones
So shall give it no concern,
To it our backs we shall not turn
Take it as a gift,
Hope is irresistible with this
So much more to see, more to do,
More to, so much more to learn

LEXICON

You do not need to climb the many steps that unevenly wind high around the guarded towers of Academia, nor do you need to meaninglessly endure inglorious rites of passage, venture on archaic perilous quests, or even practice the electronic arts of modern wizardry to possess this, the Lexicon, last of the magic books.

In its millions it still exists, often forgotten and overlooked in the cluttered dwellings of us busy mortals, and under the ghostly grey of gathering dust, that haunts the lesser travelled corridors of our monolithic emporiums.

How strange that such power should be so neglected, when new editions continuously extend its dominion.

It weighs no more than any average bound text, yet contains in their elemental forms, almost every book ever written. It holds wisdom possibly wider than any other; broadening the narrow fields in which we will choose to toil, and opening many of the doors that never should have been shut.

It translates and creates, offering opportunities that once seemed only a dream. It spells out the raw ingredients to summon up the courage, the confidence that curiosity so often needs. And with its faithful companion Thesaurus, the multi headed beast, grants protection from malevolent forces that seek to control and suppress, with sleek misdirection weaved within the suffocating mists of uncertainty's contorted labyrinth.

So, drink in its rich elixir, and forever be transformed. Unending is the power of the Lexicon, last of the magic books.

THE RIVEN HEART OF
MY MEGALOMANIA

In the open was the answer, there the method, the clarity. If we want to win the eternal battle for life to peacefully exist, then the pacifist must hit first, and must hit hardest.

If only I could write for long enough, write wide enough, intricate and plain, all towards this beautiful objective, then maybe, just maybe I could right the world.

But deep I soon fell, into the riven heart of my megalomania, the cyclone of its intended benevolence. Manifestos torn, split, broken far to quick, by the unremitting hunger of the chainsaw.

Yet in my most hopeful times, my peaceful imaginations, I am still lucid. And from such invaluable, indestructible places, we can find our serenity, if only together we are willing to step towards it.

A FEW THINGS TO REMEMBER

Our insignificance is
only an illusion.

We may be worlds apart,
but we effect each other's
with every measure
of our existence.

Anytime can be our
inception to re-learn,
to re-love ourselves
and each other.

Love like the universe
needs it. it needs its.

What ever the
wilderness, love is
what will sustain us.

Sentient, we are the same.
Love is the language that
links us, the advancement
of our code, our species.

How sweet a victory
compassion gives.

How quickly hostility
subsides when friendship
finds a way to out flank it.

You are not perfect. what
you can achieve, has
no limit, or measure.

Let hope be drawn
from your efforts
extent, and strength
from your kindness.

Without you, we are less.

With you, we are so much, we are so much more!

❖ ❖ ❖

Thank you for taking the time to read this book. If you would care to rate, or review it, I would be most grateful for your feedback.
Kind regards, Denizen Clay

Printed in Great Britain
by Amazon

22482959R00088